# the spirit level

# the
# spirit level

DAVID BARBER

TRIQUARTERLY BOOKS
NORTHWESTERN UNIVERSITY PRESS

EVANSTON, ILLINOIS

TriQuarterly Books
Northwestern University Press
Evanston, Illinois 60208-4210

Copyright © 1995 by David Barber
Published 1995 by TriQuarterly Books/
Northwestern University Press
All rights reserved

Printed in the United States of America

ISBN 0-8101-5023-9 CLOTH
ISBN 0-8101-5024-7 PAPER


Library of Congress Cataloging-in-Publication Data

Barber, David, date.
    The spirit level / David Barber.
        p.    cm.
    ISBN 0-8101-5023-9. — ISBN 0-8101-5024-7
(paper)
        I. Title.
    PS3552.A59194S65    1995
    811'.54—dc20                                95-31659
                                                    CIP

*There would still remain the never-resting mind,*
*So that one would want to escape, come back*
*To what had been so long composed.*
*The imperfect is our paradise.*
*Note that, in this bitterness, delight,*
*Since the imperfect is so hot in us,*
*Lies in flawed words and stubborn sounds.*

Wallace Stevens, "The Poems of Our Climate"


*Home-made, home-made! But aren't we all?*

Elizabeth Bishop, "Crusoe in England"

# Contents

III

# Acknowledgments

The author would like to thank the editors of the following publications, in which some of these poems, or earlier versions, first appeared:

*Agni*: "Ladies of the Necropolis," "Memo on the Hereafter," "My Quarrel with Queen Anne's Lace"

*Atlantic Monthly*: "The Lather"

*Boulevard*: "Mysteries of the Deep"

*Button*: "Barnum in Nantucket"

*Antioch Review*: "First Light, False Dawn"

*Georgia Review*: "The Earth Is Round"

*Gettysburg Review*: "An American Sampler," "The Threshers"

*Graham House Review*: "Dawn of the Atom"

*Ironwood*: "Nocturne"

*Missouri Review*: "Small Hours," "Sudden Clarity at the Artichoke Stands"

*New England Review*: "'American Forest Scene: Maple Sugaring'" (part III of "Three Scenes from Currier & Ives")

*New Republic*: "Autumnal Primer"
*New Voices* (7th ed.): "Under Gemini"

*North American Review*: "The Dark Ages"

*Paris Review*: "Dürer's Rhinoceros"

*Partisan Review*: "The Spirit Level"

*Ploughshares*: "Elegy for the Bad Uncles,"
"Prospectus"

*Poetry*: "The Favor," "Little Overture"

*Poetry Northwest*: "South," "Studebaker Luck"

*Sonora Review*: "Worldly Goods"

*Southwest Review*: "Apocrypha After Dark"

*TriQuarterly*: "Lines on a Yankee Aphorism,"
"Zooms and Pans"

Grateful acknowledgment is also extended to the MacDowell
Colony for a residency in 1994; to PEN New England for a
PEN Discovery Award presented in 1991; to the Massachusetts
Artists Foundation for a Fellowship grant awarded in 1988;
and to Stanford University and the Academy of American Poets
for two University Prizes awarded in 1985 and 1986. Lastly,
many thanks to Reginald Gibbons and Susan Hahn for their
acute insights and sage counsels.

*I*

# The Lather

On the tin stowed under the upstairs sink
The mule team circulates in silhouette,
Yeoman hand-scrub of workingmen and sons
Going back to before his father was born.

And so he pictures vast bleached dunes
Shimmering to the vanishing point,
The chalky powder heaped in mounds
And hauled to the city by wagon train

To meet demand, a grand procession.
So let tar bleed from telephone poles,
Let engine-blocks ooze rainbow slicks
And bike-chains jam with caked-up gunk—

He's heard his father say one scoop will cut
Through any crap, no matter what,
Just work the lather good, keep at it.
He's fallen into rhythm now, a little remote,

A little dreamy: the team marches round
The tin like ants, his wrists turn and turn
In a reaming motion, and his head spins
To think of all the pitch-black hands

Squelching away at this dinner hour,
Filling washbasins with oily rivers.
And now his suds froth even darker.
His skin's on fire. He feels certain

The storied mines can't last forever:
The dunes will dwindle into moondust,
The mules will litter the desert floor
With hollow skulls. He knows in his bones

He's turning into the kind of upstart
Who never misses a chance to flout
A father's orders about what not to touch
Or take apart. In the fogging mirror

He sees himself far older, doubled over
Fiendish smears that won't rinse out
(Some industrial taint? Indelible ink?)
Faithfully, furiously though he scours.

# The Spirit Level

You kept your tools sequestered,
out of sight. And to this day, the flinty logic
    of the ratchet and the crescent
wrench evades me, I'm unable to brandish
    a saw or drive a batch of penny nails
without a passing twinge of sheepishness.
    But the spirit level, let me tell you,
is another story: so ingenious in the essence
    of its unvarnished purpose, it's practically
child's play. Yours was as long as your arm:
    a perfect makeshift shotgun for a boy
like me. But slipping downstairs first thing
    Sunday mornings, bent on infiltrating
the inspired clutter of your basement sanctum,
    I found it even more ingratiating
for what it was, for how its stripped-down upshot
    was both transparent and inscrutable.
Winking in their banded tubes of tinted glass,
    those emerald bubbles never burst
or vanished, no matter how savagely I shook
    or how doggedly I worked to tilt
and drown them. It seemed to me there had
    to be some clever dodge concealed
in its sundry uses, like umbrellas that sheath
    a well-honed blade, or the dining
table's folded wings. Still, such artfulness
    as I could grasp held all the thrill
of uncanny scorcery: the fingernail flecks
    of captive air always at the ready,
the stringent tension, streamlined to divine
    absolute vertical, true horizontal,

the furtive thrust of angles. Did I ever
    tell you that the basement floor
slumped faintly, here and there, the beams
    betrayed a hair's-breadth slant?
Did I already tell you that every doorframe
    would make those bubbles tremble,
as if the house were just then beginning
    to sink down on one knee?

# First Light, False Dawn

So you see, it is useless.
Where there are wings, I have

days and years on my hands,
and the persuasive sadness

of unmatching dishes washed
unfailingly each night

until they shone like so many moons.
I can see her face in every one

as a flash of local color,
while above her head

another prize of Audubon's
in its native tree or thicket

seems to contemplate flight.
Accept and forgive, fall and rise,

how else does the passage of time
instruct us? Chairs go round

the table, the dishtowel moves
in circles, the moon steals

over the house. And come morning,
on many occasions, I've clapped

my hands under telephone wires,
on the margins of fields,

and the larks and starlings
hurtling upwards were pages

for an unfinished book of hours.
And in spring the swallows return,

the fishing boats shove off
at dawn, shadowed by a wedding-train

of gulls. If I am unmoved,
I have learned well. I grew up

in a house where little was said,
where a woman lost her will

and beauty in the usual mild ways:
task by task, day by untold day.

Where high above the kitchen sink
in our perennial calendar

sleek plovers preened,
an oriole sang, and the snow goose

craned its neck skyward
while others streamed by overhead.

# Nocturne

The papers say the heat is here to stay.
Every window in the house thrown open
to a child's durable choruses.
He should be sung to. All of us should be.
The one good lullaby my mother knew
harbored a line in the distance darker
than the others, processions of ridges.
Some were scored with horses, or so I heard.

And I seem to recall braids of smoke, towns
in the strongholds of rivers, those slow blues.
But I could be mistaken. As children,
we wake in what we come to call the woods.
No faces, no dim outlines of bodies.
No lacework of stars: the trees are that thick.
Only a strand of song, that one refrain
that could still the eyelids at midsummer.

Nights I can't sleep, I know my mother sings.
I stray outdoors in hopes of hearing her.
There are the towns and there are the horses.
And there's a road I must have missed before.
Chimneys ghost on; ladles chime off kettles.
A local cradling kindling shuffles by
with a nod, whistling ferociously.
It isn't summer here. It never was.

# Zooms and Pans

What hope did we ever have against the virtual?
Where's the will that might have jammed the spell?
The ball glides under the outstretched glove
with an immaculate serenity we couldn't have dreamed,

the hook shot swoons and rips the net,
the uppercut sends the thickly aging champion
into the annals of cauliflowered oblivion
from seven elegant and omniscient angles.

The shivering crossbar, the sandtrap save,
the unparalleled pike, the textbook bunt—
in the booth there are knobs and buttons,
men expressly wired to convert dubious commotion

into sequences rich and epic, fixed beyond dispute,
instilling the sense at last that our bodies too,
rewound in avid slo-mo, would surely disclose
a telling pivot or a clinching move.

The father and son have scarcely budged a muscle.
The game wears on. The season ends today.
Their hearts belong to the side in red and gold,
the father's school. The son is small but knows

the rules like catechism, knows the mechanics
of erupting heroics and the stratagems
essential to offset the accidents of fortune.
And when the quarterback wheels and completes a rocket

or when the ball squirts free like a wet seed
or when two lunging bodies meet savagely in midair,
he knows why the screen must run it over: the revealing,
the lingering, the penetrating second look.

Doesn't it figure he'll come to spend hours eluding
hordes of phantom tacklers in a honeyed trance?
Or in fiendish playground war games, to perish
in lurid slow motion, a thousand elastic deaths?

And is it so inscrutable, all those years later
in a cavernous library, that he'd snap out of a catnap
gripped by zooms and pans: Hector and Achilles
locked in tape-loop combat, an endless instant replay?

Reel to reel, it can all be reprised.
So that what appeared to be time's arrow
becomes just one in a series of peregrinations
under the law of averages, the going odds.

Reel to reel: the split-second before contact,
the hairtrigger hipshake after the handoff,
the spiral's wobble and the juggled grab.
So that what's left are trajectories, various stories

streamlined by the technology of memory.
Any moment now (*run it over*) the star will plunge
into the line to seal the win, the son will lean
closer this time, dipping under that slack arm.

# Elegy for the Bad Uncles

Hands the likes of which
We'll never know again
Have grasped us, found us

Everything they wished for
As an answer to the body's
Tendency toward mass

And ponderous desire.
So it was only natural
That they would want

To hoist us as far away
From the earth as possible—
Closer to lamplight, starlight,

Or the scalloped clouds
At the windowpane
Like worked gold leaf.

Oh, we were masterful.
We spun there above
The upturned faces,

The shining china
And Christmas goose,
The indignant lapdogs,

As if all light and luck
Might somehow owe
Their origins to us

And who were we
To say it wasn't so?
We didn't disappoint them:

We let those hands
Have their way with us
Despite the unspeakable acts

In unthinkable battles
Or in the rooms of
Unmentionable women

That had stained them.
We cannot blame them,
Even now, for feeling

Cleansed or merely
Forgiven, for holding us
Up to the heavens

Far longer than they
Earlier intended, before
Lowering us reluctantly

To others, or down at last
To the level of their own
Disreputable hearts.

# The Span

The acoustics of the place
Were such that murmurs carried
And a boy could sound like God

By uncorking a quick shout.
Amplified beneath an arch
Like that, a gurgling ditch

Will roar, any footfall
Echo and a quarrel
Among a band of three

Assume in memory
An operatic pitch,
A bodily vibrato.

Suicide Bridge, the townsfolk
Dubbed it, hotspot
For leapers, foolproof—

But for us, its underbelly
Was less a catacomb
Than some imperial vault:

Conspiratorially dark
No matter the time of day,
A delectably covert

Base camp and fountainhead
In all its slimy glory,
A bottle-shattering heaven,

Frog rookery come spring,
And every outcry booming
Like an exhortation in

The bosom of a church
Or the lubadub of a heart
Heard through a stethoscope.

Did I say a quarrel?
Now that I listen closely
I find I am mistaken:

This is no scrap or donnybrook—
It is my coronation.
No wonder the room's a drum;

No wonder my pulse races.
The winning mayonnaise jar
Is mine, the verdict sealed

With lusty claps of thunder.
Now the streets are ice.
The world turns on its side.

Take it from a king
Of the frogs, a monarch
Emeritus of a culvert:

The clamor is never
Out of earshot, no matter
How sundered, how riven,

How forsaken the sources.
When the past throws its voice,
I lose all sense of scale:

That span's like a ship
In a bottle, a delicate
Artifact, an intricate feat

Of painstaking detail
And distilled perspective.
Everything intact, each touch

Emblematic: the Day-Glo
Who's who of local toughs,
The bobbing rubbers

Like shucked frogskin,
Shell-cases and pill-boxes,
The middens of hoboes.

Even the air-raid horn
Tuning up on schedule,
Like a wasp-drone on glass.

# The Divided City

Many of us still remember how it began as idle pleasure.
The afternoons spooled out, our blood sugars bubbled over,
History hadn't been invented yet. We loved how warm
The stones felt in our hands, how firm their marbled shapes.

We were no more or less than boys. Our language was our own.
The California sun had already turned us brown or red
Before the school year ended. We drifted home in bands,
Rainbowing granite wedges downslope into underbrush.

We were hardly thinking in those days. The motion alone
Must have won us over: aimless slinging, easy lobs.
But before we knew it, we were judging distances too well.
It came entirely naturally. Our wrists were built to snap.

Perhaps you heard the glorious clatter as we winged the names
Of presidents and eminent trees: Washington and Cherry,
Willow, Lincoln, and Ash. Perhaps you were wondering
Why the arc lamps on your street kept going dark.

How many of us were bad seeds? Impossible to tell.
If you believe the murmurings, there are changelings
The upright incubate unwittingly in any given populace.
Dead-eyed, we found the range. It happened much too fast.

The wire services froze one of us at the moment of release
And it flashed around the world. Now that forces dwarf us,
Our unrest is news—our grainy hailstorms are in demand.
That's us with the swaddled faces. The ones with pumping arms.

Our shortcuts through backlots now lead to market districts
Where no eyes meet. It's up to packs of our kind to keep
The enclaves at their throats, the outbreaks symptomatic.
We're as young as ever, but now our enmities are ancient.

Many of us keep forgetting exactly where we are.
Satellite feeds beam holy wars into our rooms.
Look for me through the wrong end of the telescope:
Skulking in the landscaped dusk, loading up with rocks.

# Mysteries of the Deep

Because the artist was scrupulous
    not to tip the scales or take sides,
because the depiction aimed to capture
    the most titanic encounter
science and fancy could agree on,
    the giant squid and the sperm whale
will be forever locked together
    in my mind, in my desire
to reconcile myself to a double helix
    of passion and transgression;

because the rain was unappeasable
    that day, because I'd been entrusted
with my solitude all afternoon
    out of desperate expediency
as recriminations swarmed at home,
    the library seemed the ideal diving bell
and I the ideal child to man
    a descent into the tacit hush
of forbidding seas, to plumb the realm
    of voluptuous and tumescent monsters;

because the color plate betrayed
    no hint of an outcome,
because it was beyond me to conceive
    of what might possibly transpire
once the immense mouth snapped shut
    and the flaring tentacles took grip,
I am left with a decision that hangs
    in the balance, an apotheosis

of an embrace, a mobius of yes and no,
    relinquishment and vanquishment;

because who would I be deceiving
    if I turned the page, if I swallowed
that child whole, scuttled that first sensation
    of convoluted otherness;
because why else do the two of us
    vie on the bed in a primal knot
but to test our powers as unquenchable creatures;
    because who would wish to choose
between the heartstopping stranglehold
    and the belly of the beast?

# Worldly Goods

The fan opens

over her lap. This is the backward glance.
            The late afternoon of her childhood.
The bend in the river, flowering plum,

the mouth of the fishmonger
            a bellows of song. One hairpin crane
spiking the rushes, one hardy waterman

throwing every sinew into keeping
            his leaf of a craft on line, out where
the current has a mind of its own.

This is how the inner life
            is brought to light, a membrane
of memory, a fluent blueprint.

See how the bridge arcs
            just so, like a hand held curved
above the brow, the better to peer

into the burnished neighboring
            province, to scan and take in
the next bright rib? See how

its span embraces the horizon,
            the seagoing sails like fireflies
hovering just an eyelash below

the couriers' sandaled feet?
          This is what forms us. The far
and the near. The sense of nothing

left out. And here's where inferences
          take over: you must imagine the village
in the east and the village

in the west, now that it's flared
          like a bird's wing. You must trust her:
no vast distance, as the crane flies,

nothing backbreaking, as you
          can tell from the milling harmony
of this high road, stout merchants lifting

dimpled arms out of brilliant
          flagged sleeves in simultaneous
greeting and farewell. Look,

that one has a comb in his hair
          and this one has secured a tiny,
handsome cricket cage

to the side of his pack. A gift
          for his daughter, she felt certain,
a souvenir of the silk route.

What a rakish smile. It grows
          on you. No wonder he drew her
like a steady flame,

his grand staff and glad step
        so unswerving with dovetailing
flourish and purpose

as to render all but invisible
        the still one under the feathery willow
near the pinch of the hinge. For years

she never noticed him,
        the one who must be a sage,
there, in the steeping blue shade

with his rice-paper scrolls. Whose pair
        of astonishing silver mustaches
must have tested the finest brush

and who, if a traveler
        were to kneel beside him before
crossing over, would utter

strange, unfathomable truths:
        how appearances deceive,
how the leaping pike will never return

to its weedy floating world
        and the dragonfly will elude
the harrowing kingfisher forever

(but barely, just barely)
        and how behind this scudding sky
the heavens fashion a woman's face,

her eyes open.

*II*

# An American Sampler

This was how to rebuke the devils
Who poach upon the fair and idle.
A strip of linen, an essential stitch,
Intimacy with needle and silk.

A girl's education was consummated
In alphabets and inscriptions.
Custom circumscribed the scenes:
Streamlined townships, homespun Edens.

In the colonies geometry lost ground.
The bluebird throve, and the snaking vine
Lavishly girdled the given psalm.
The redskin's gourd left thumbprints of orange.

Gone the pinched English margins.
Gone the sparse pastels. Bowers and gardens
Annexed the proper band and scalloped edge.
Borders crept inward and grew bold.

Hannah Abbott's china roses are crimped
With satin for convincing depth.
She's adorned her dainty seated figure
With actual amber hair. The green fire

Of a willow doubles as an alcove,
Just the spot to pine for one's beloved.
Here the wilderness no longer howls:
Pillowy clouds of sheep and speckled cows

Bob on the fledgling nation's rolling knolls.
A girl could stroll there free of peril,
Blackberrying perhaps. She's worked them right
Into her sky, clusters large as life.

# Barnum in Nantucket

Here's the rub:
the Republic's archetypal shark
was just another rube
that afternoon, a gaping epigone
caught up in Leviathan's maw.

Was he awestruck? Delectable
to think him so. Here was a jaw
wide as a double churchdoor,
grand as a robber baron's balustrade,
a spectacle that spoke for itself.

A certain Captain Cash,
an island salt, had overcome the monster.
And now its implausible bleached smile
loomed in the tallowworks
like a prodigious lucky horseshoe.

Or was it a wishbone? Never mind.
In his book, courting fortune
couldn't hold a candle
to burning the midnight oil,
to banking on a silver tongue.

Back on the mainland
the impresario dispatched a letter
(encouraged, no doubt,
by the sensible ring
of the good captain's name)

proposing that the breathtaking
artifact be donated at once
to "a grateful posterity"—
"or if you don't see it
in that light . . .

whether you will sell it
to be placed in my museum
and if so, at what price."
No deal was struck.
How it must have stuck

in his craw, a sensation like that
marooned on a flyspeck—
while on the blazing thoroughfares
his countrymen by the millions
swarmed like so many minnows.

# The Dark Ages

Half a century from now the boy whose face
is penny-radiant between the smoking lanterns
will not remember the name of the bear.

And he will not remember which slow waltz
the piano hammered out, though he will know
it was familiar and blamed some crime on the moon.

On the other side of the river, an open window
is waiting for him. A chinaberry tree
is forking under the sill. The room will be

smaller when he finally crawls back in
and come morning the bedsheets will smell
of tobacco and kerosene. And whiskey, somehow.

And the world will tilt toward poverty and war.
But here and now he's trying to understand
why everybody's jeering, why the eyes of the bear

are bloodshot and glassy, as if pricked by tears.
Her ankle-shackle and string of pearls shine.
There are men in the throng who outweigh her.

And when she weaves and lurches like a
punchdrunk fighter, the laughter swells in time;
sawdust rises and swirls and the gold tooth

of the piano player gleams. It will seem
to the boy, a lifetime later, that the bear
was on fire, that at any given moment

his own face might have burst into flames.
He will not remember the names on the handbills
but on summer nights he will tell his grandchildren

that when he was young every full moon
was a scorching lump of coal above the freightyards
and men and beasts alike danced for their lives.

# Dürer's Rhinoceros

*[1515]*

The imagination, improvising, translated burly leather
into an overcoat of armor, converted brawn to iron.
For wrinkled folds, die-tooled metal plates
secured with welded struts. For mottled hide,
stamped medallions and, bellywise, rippling bursts
like sunspots Galileo's glass would mark a century hence.
A submarine should be riveted so impeccably.
A Swiss vault should be this stoutly tamperproof.

Chimerical and mechanical, one foot in biology
and the other in technology, Europe's debut rhino
poses on a patch of stylized turf, outsize toenails
planted squarely at the crosshatched intersection
of hearsay, surmise, awe, and steely virtuosity.
Making the most of slender evidence, the Master erred
on the side of industrial-strength intimidation:
spiked shanks, serrated hindquarters, vulcanized anatomy.

Where brute facts are lacking, exactitude takes refuge
in preternatural convictions. Here, the prevailing temper
called for ornament to shade into armament;
ascertained a galvanizing center of gravity
in a lordly girth; branded the newfangled implacable.
Here, the spirit of revelation elevated the nubby backup horn
to an exalted position, plucked from the creature's snout
and stuck between the shoulder blades, a crowning touch.

Did he clank when he walked? Could he so much as twitch
his mistakenly furry ears under all that battlegear?

Let us not dare to read the mind of the Almighty.
The chronicles only tell us he was to be a king's gift
to the Pope, an impenetrable marvel doomed to perish
in a shipwreck en route to Rome. Lost to the deeps,
he's already a full-blown apparition in the woodcut—
a wonder reconstructed, a secondhand stab at a likeness.

Palm-frond tail, barnacled jowl, muttonchops of bony matter—
no question, he's more than a little clownish, our poor
tinhorn monster: a bulky hyperbole, a Falstaff on all fours.
Oh, but look him up and down, and it's amply evident
allegedness has worked a certain alchemy on him.
Shackle or tether would be superfluous: his fearsomeness
has gone the way of all flesh, all this staggering regalia
houses a will-o'-the-wisp. Lapidary in its declivity,

his one eye's neither wary nor bellicose. In the shop,
he scanned sinewy fallen angels harvesting lost souls.
Inked into his element, the perspective is reversed,
and he broods, a dour nightwatchman, on the prickly heavens.
He's built to outlast edicts and categorical imperatives.
Taxonomy can't touch him now. His burden's to be wise
to the whispers that he's altogether otherworldly,
he who was immortalized as a champion of the earthbound.

# Dawn of the Atom

*St. George, Utah, 1953*

It was pink as a cat's tongue, pink as the erasers
we chewed on during arithmetic.

It was the pink of India on the creaking library globe.

It was confetti, it was fairy dust, it was just as if
it was everybody's birthday.

By noon the bus drivers were using their wipers.
There was a powdering of pink on the policeman's cap,
a film of pink in the bird fountains,

pink cake-crumbs piping the cracks in the pavement.

On the radio an especially fuzzy static,
as if the flakes were clotting the air waves:
something about the success of a test,
something about the world's powers.

By mid-afternoon the crosswalks were disappearing,
our hopscotch squares were smudging away, the names
on the awnings were nearly indecipherable.

It was the pink of lipstick and lemonade:
the shade of lipstick our mothers wore on Easter,
the fountain glasses of pink lemonade
we slurped through candy-striped straws.

It was New Year's Day, it was Mardi Gras, it was as if
the whole town had turned out for a wedding.

On the radio, more crackling: mild and sunny
for tomorrow, a chance of an evening shower
and a hot spell expected for the weekend

but no mention of the pink half-moons under lampposts,
no word of the pink rivers in the gutters,
that was ours alone, we were the lucky ones.

And we filled our pockets and lunchboxes.
It glittered in our hair. We drew hearts and faces
on the hoods of cars, we signed our names.

We chased our pink dogs home through frosted streets.

So that even when the winds died down
by nightfall, we were still the dazzling children
the skies had singled out to strew with favors—

pink as bubble-gum, pink as doll's cheeks, pink
as the roses gaping on our bedroom walls.

# Three Scenes from Currier & Ives

Picture-book drifts. Windswept standstill.
No sign of the heavens; no cinders
Shooting in the funnel's smoke-pour.
The engine-lamp burns its midnight oil.
The tender's half-sunk
Like a sleeper's chin in a feather pillow.
Late the vaunted Express.
Late, late the hour.
            And back in the coaches
Fading into the curve and out of the frame,
Gloves must be rubbing peepholes
On the breath-steamed glass.
Can anyone spot the sickle moon?
Has anyone spied the conductor's watchchain?
Can this possibly be America,
This forest primeval, this trackless landscape
Out of the pages of a penny-dreadful?
And how would the heroine carry on,
Pray tell? The firs are twisting
Into tortured figures before her eyes.
Her crinoline gnashes as she cranes.
Her father's gone to join the others
Digging out the rails like roughnecks
In a salt mine, but she's lost him
Amid the fists and false beards smoke makes
As winter gusts blow out the stars.

## 2. "TROLLING FOR BLUE FISH"

Students of the new translucency
Could work with this sky:
Touch of rose in the cloud-roll;
Near shoreline, a hint of lavender.

But in the foreground all's aboil.
Serious chop, the sail bellying.
The sea's a livid thing today.

Tillerman: mind that starboard list.
Your triumvirate of paying gentlemen
Are inescapably possessed.
A run of bluefish does that to a soul.
A fever-tide inflames the blood.

Full beard, slouch hat, burly frame—
You could be another Renoir, Monet.
Your jaw's a rock. It seems to say
This party of swells will be your last.

No more will you set a trusty course
Across this bruising pitch and toss.
Let other pilots work the kill.
Let other purses gulp the spoils.

Don't look back, man. Sell the sloop.
Take up brushes, steam overseas.
You know from the rainbows
On your hands that light
Swarms over us in particles
Like scattered fishscales.
The sky is never blue.

It's the past that's lost beyond all reckoning
That steeps to an innermost sweetness.
Childhood, the old ways, laughter pealing
In a woodland glade cleared ages ago
For roads that look like a diagram of nerves
From the air. If the engraver knows
Anything, it's this: one can't go wrong
In the vein of distilled nostalgia,
Proverbial innocence, halcyon overtones.

Therefore, the boy who daydreams near the kettle
That's rendering an ambrosia of premium amber
Wears his little hauling-yoke lightly, jauntily,
As if it were a hovering memory already.
Naturally, he's a sturdy lad: his apple cheeks
Can't hide the outlines of a manly bearing.
He's fetched the buckets from the faithful taps
Without letting spill so much as a drop.
All his elders are sure that he'll go far
In this life—his name's on their lips
As they mind the fire in the center of the print.
Next year they'll show him how to wield the axe,
Which even now is jutting from a fallen trunk
And gesturing like an angel's extended arm
Back out of the glade, into open country.

# Heaven and Earth

*"I play piano, but God is in the house tonight."*
—*Fats Waller, on Art Tatum*

All the fountains in the city, all the heirloom pitchers
and teacups and decanters in fashionable kitchens
and all the lagoons and millponds on the estates
across the Sound could not contain the torrents

when the big man hit his stride. Like love, like justice,
his blindness was profound, his unerring ear a wonder,
and all through his late set the shabby baby grand
opened up like the heavens, drowning the stars.

And the gutters would overflow, the streets would hiss.
The new moon tucked crisply into a classic wick
above his heart. All of Harlem's tears, all the beads
of honest sweat in boiler rooms and chophouses

and every drop knocked back in firetrap dives
paled beside the grace notes those bearish hands
would pour into a wispy ballad or a cornpone show tune
as the after-hours regulars began to throng.

It's said a soul couldn't help but light up the place
with another fine row of ivories in the rollcall
of lightning arpeggios. It's said the angels listened in.
Cakewalks surging into dambursts, blues into Niagaras:

a cadenza can churn the bloodstream into froth,
a rising tide will lift all bodies. Nobody called it faith

to its face, but that must have been the unspoken theme—
the inescapable impression, at daybreak, swaying home

to the cold-water flats, that the sky was blushing,
that any quarter flooded with such harmonies
would some day be washed clean of all ill will
and quiet desperation, streets shining and lapels in bloom.

# Lines on a Yankee Aphorism

*"The tongue is ever turning to the aching tooth."*

The face exacts its creases, even as you speak.
The cowlick springs back smartly from the smoothing touch.
The tongue is ever turning to the aching tooth.

The elbow stiffens in cold snaps, where once it cracked
On account of a rotting beech, a rankling taunt.
The hand balls up again, as if the jibe were fresh.

The tunes return at intervals, snatches at a time:
Sponsors' jingles, beery choruses, martial strains.
He'd fiercely whistle along. It set your teeth on edge.

The customary card arrives, that jagged hand:
"Blessings of the season from the bottom of my heart."
The tongue is ever turning to the aching tooth.

The manhandled file drawers routinely jam.
There's not a pencil in the desk that isn't gnawed.
The diminutive nickname sticks—you bite your tongue.

The woeful porch-step rounds into pitch each muddy spring.
Was ever there a harkening any sweeter to your ear?
Is this the footfall that will finally break its back?

The dusk's astir with summer insects, a soft white noise.
Their wings prick at your cheeks and pluck your eyes.
It will not taper off. It drives you back inside.

The smiles in the photo album glint like hooks.
This one's jokes would always end in coughs and oaths.
That one's smoke rings took a lifetime to perfect.

The squint once doubled as a wink. The fluttering tic
Entered the world as a winning flicker of delight.
The tongue is ever turning to the aching tooth.

The razor scrapes away; the mock scent of lemon
Will linger on your neck all morning like bad faith.
The jaw goes tight; the brow's a divot; the lashes glisten.

The blackened thumbnail restores itself to rosy pink.
The long bright scar grows fainter every time you look.
And still the mouth throbs. And still the tongue works.

# My Quarrel with Queen Anne's Lace

Come summer, on wayside knolls,
in postage-stamp cemeteries
          and abandoned boatyards,
I lay myself down, I vanish completely

          under the finery and swaying mirth
of that embrace. And I say,
          very softly, that this must end—
the license, the largesse, the prolific

          incandescence, and the temerity
to court neglect incessantly
          as if nothing were more worthy
of such longing. And I say

          it isn't so, it can't be done,
the life of fullness and promise
          shall not redound to us
simply by wedding unflagging desire

          to wild generosity, not even
sustaining loveliness, lasting consolation.
          Your rush to caress backlots,
failed gardens, dirt-poor meadows,

          only deceives us. Your wish
that pastures where the stables burned
          might brighten and sweeten again,
so soon, alarms. And I say

ambition and compassion
must not be confounded:
        to be half as ardent, nearing
August, would be to move us

        twice as artfully. And I rise
at last, wade back to the road.
        I hug the curves towards home
through the murmur and glimmer of fields.

# Prospectus

I am working on a field guide to wind.
It will be my labor of love, my legacy.
None of us should have to countenance
A loss of words, a lack of common names
In the face of the world's embarrassing wealth
Of sundry motions and stirrings.

I am working on a source in which
Each large and small disturbance of the air
Will be found between two covers.
It will be the definitive text, the gospel.
No naturalist will want to live without one,
No serious novelist will underestimate its worth.

The colored plates will be magnificent:
Billowing spinnakers and rippling flags,
The languorous exhalations of curtains
Before an open kitchen window.
In the unexpurgated edition, summer dresses
Will swirl jubilantly above the thighs.

The margins will boast inspired sketches
Of weathervanes and windchimes, top hats
Evading recapture, surefire ways to measure
The tug on your sleeve, the chill in the hall.
There will be appendices appraising airsocks
And windbags. The rise and fall of dragon kites.

Blasts, gusts, squalls, drafts and flurries,
The families of breezes, the lives of whispers:
I'm busy cataloging every fit and eddy.

For scholars, there will be a vast concordance
Of atmospheric pressures. For amateurs,
An easy key to ill winds that blow no good.

I am working on an inventory of unrest,
A compendium of perennial nods and shudders.
It will be my tour de force, my masterpiece.
Yesterday's newspaper snags in the forsythia.
The garden gate ticks softly; the peach tree shivers.
I'm filling whole pages with gasps and sighs.

# Little Overture

A shimmering in the scrub-brush
Beside the tracks, a pleasing silken weft
Of stray raiment amid the rubbish.

Grace is like this: a scrim
Materializing in a strip of stubbly weeds.
It comes, it goes, a glint, a form

Of counterpoint and seduction.
Or call it a sampler, the handiwork
Of spring's first spiders practicing deception.

Now come closer. If it's silver lining
You want, it seems you have been hoodwinked.
Knots of kids have strewn

The slick innards of unspooled cassettes
Over the brambles as they wended
Home from school along the tracks.

Whose loss is it? Grace is like this.
Railway perennials shine in the wind.
Threads recur; pop songs persist

In telling us what we wish were true.
Trains storm by on time but still you wander,
Nodding to a beat you cannot hear.

# Ladies of the Necropolis

Ferret of the imperial library, laureate of prurience,
Suetonius survives in codexes of scuttlebutt,
vigorous discourses on character defects,
biographical sketches distilled to a quintessence
of fizzy hearsay. On the emperors
he is prolix, fiendish, and sublimely nosy:
no depravity of Nero's too negligible,
no repugnancy of Caligula's too nominal,
for his taste in lapidary innuendo.

Lost to us are reams of his lowdown
and chitchat, the lion's share of his eclectic output.
Alas, my fellow enthusiasts of dissolute arcana,
his exhaustive treatise on Greek profanity
nowhere awaits our moistened index fingers;
nor are we able to troll for instructive corollaries
in his inventory of the ever more outré apparel
a crumbling empire comes to fancy.
Worse yet, we're to be forever deprived of frittering
a rainy afternoon away in the reading room
with his *Lives of Eminent Courtesans,*
which you may have taken the liberty, of course,
to translate as *The Lives of Notable Concubines*
or *The True Confessions of Renowned Prostitutes*
or, if you savored that touch of Roman coarseness,
perhaps *The Rise and Fall of Famous Whores.*
The choice is yours; the work has perished,
and in its place we are entitled to plant
the rambling tendrils of conjecture, a grapevine
of concupiscent speculation and editorial license,
here in the stacks where the classics repose.

As for me, I have already determined
that it must have been his magnum opus.
What better project for a quidnunc?
What finer way to heed the voyeuristic impulse
lurking in every true archivist than to embark
on a little unsung history of the flesh?
The scholars agree that above all our scribe
coveted obsessive detail, so you see, my divagations
are perfectly limitless. I can have him
listing the unguents stirred into a pre-tryst bath.
I can have him sneering over the twaddle
statesmen have been known to burp and mumble
into a creamy shoulder. I can have him
tallying brushstrokes, pearled combs, rows of plaits;
goblets drained, gouges dealt, deceptions gilded;
hours of business, years of service.
Some would be contemptuous; some wistful;
all would turn weary in time. The pages throng.
The profession was ancient even then.

Paramours of Suetonius! Lend me your ears!
Your amanuensis has never been mistaken
for an epochal conscience or a moral zealot.
I am persuaded that he saw in you
no rampant scourge or parasitic civic vice
but a surpassing glossary of carnal knowledge,
a testament to dispassionate enterprise,
case studies in the eternal push and shove
between vanity's dictates and priapic verities.
Not that I wish for a moment to ennoble him:
if I know my gadfly, I'll wager he milked you
for raunch and titillation at every turn,
lingering with oily alacrity over every wet spot
he espied. And I can only begin to surmise

by what criteria he deemed you illustrious,
whether your worthiness was clinched by indexing
your charms and wiles, your stamina and prowess,
or what's more likely, your lasting esteem
as the favorites among the fat cats.

All this is to say that I've convinced myself
that you should thank your assorted gods and stars
for seeing to it the text was filed in the void
and none of you was handed down intact,
replete with coifs and potions, warts and all.
Every so often, I imagine, a fumbling old goat
grew so inflamed as to compare you to the sylphs,
and now—*sic transit!*—it's come to pass,
for you are all spirit, all fragrant air
and evanescent supposition. Your debauches
the stuff of ashes, steamy fleshpot tricks
no longer, you're free to hover above us
as you wish, and we cannot patronize you.
In my private draft of the palimpsest, I confess,
you've been elevated into a redoubtable tribunal
empowered to tip the scales of pleasure,
a star chamber of fair women with jurisdiction
over the welter of our crushes and arousals.
O be merciful with us as we grope and sweat,
O be munificent as you weigh in on the ache—
I know it's been ages, but the story never changes
except for the names and the faces, the slant
and the stamp of the torrid marginalia,
and the desire that demands its own imprimatur.

# Memo on the Hereafter

All the precepts of theology and chemistry
categorically proscribe it. Every loophole
serendipity affords us holds out little hope.
But I can't help it, I won't be mollified
so easily this morning: if it's heaven
I'm asked to aspire to and bear in mind,
I want the place to make room for a little rust.
Trust me, this is not my idea of impertinence
or an exercise in offhand heresy.
I'm not speaking here of pure being
crudely blighted or halos eaten away.
All I want is a dispensation of sorts.
All I'd require is a discreet stippling
off to one side, a blushing constellation,
a patch of crusty scarlet, say,
or a tiny moonscape of burgundy and sepia.
Here on earth, I don't exactly adore it,
I confess. My loyalties are mixed.
But this morning, thinking to resurrect
the dismal swatch of weedy turf
behind the house with consoling greenery,
I'm learning to admire the oxymoron
that's the soul of rust. Feverishly modest,
imperiously democratic, scrupulously discomposed,
it's worked clean through the bottom
of the watering can, throttled the shears
with cankers, caked the one good trowel.
It would turn the mower-blades into cornflakes
if I let it. It would pick the tool-shed lock.
Burnt orange, scabbed ocher, flagrant umber—
I'm not saying it's lovely, mind you,

only that it smacks of the glaring lapses
and the outbreaks that come with fallen territory,
only that it grounds us in the knowledge
that all the hard evidence we would clutch
is busy understudying thin air.
And if we are permitted to entertain a sliver
of paradise in the premeditated bloom and calm
of a backyard garden, then I say
give me a cranny in the afterlife
to sow a touch, a trace, of earthly ruin.
I say let me keep a plot of fiery streaks
and blood-drop freckles. I say let me
potter over hothouse implosions, crumbling gashes,
brittle rosettes. Grant me a memento mori
in reverse, grant me the grace of this dear rash
so I will know, with all eternity
on my hands, that I belonged once to a realm
whose overlords were patience and corrosion.

*III*

# Apocrypha After Dark

A crowd in a ring—sure, call it a throng.
A grizzled face and a milky-gray horse
in the center. I can't say which outshines

the other under the sputtering gaslights:
the star on the forehead or the scar
on that gaunt cheek. It's all I can do

to make sure we eel our way together
through the musty overcoats to the very front—
orphans, it seems, unkempt urchins

who find they've strayed to the far edge
of anywhere they might ever have dreamed up:
another century, by the looks of it.

But shush now: we are truly rapt.
The man declares the mare knows all.
He asks for volunteers: look, here we are.

It's all I can do to keep my shoulders square
and your chin firm: so picture us staunch
between the lashes of one of those wonder horses

who were all the rage in the old country
once upon a time, swayback nags who charmed
and gulled the rabble by rapping clop

for yes and clock-clop for no
or totted up sums at a tattooed clip
with the flinty accuracy of a shopkeeper.

The ruse, it's said, lay in certain signs
that would pass between master and beast,
infinitesimal gestures tipping the answers . . .

but for all I can tell, that sidelong gaze
has ably sized us up, extracting our facts
and secrets as we might bone a fish.

Unbelievably deep, this sliver of pasture-fence
would doze the summer away beneath the skin
were it not for you, bent over my palm

and worming a needle as if to darn a seam
in my fortune. Hard under the winglamp
our flesh washes out, and in my mind

the milky-gray mare we plied with crescents
of green apple has already turned legendary—
a creature out of a folk tale, it seems,

or a gaslit, sepia past where straying urchins
(are they orphans?) are fingered in a trice
to show how well a wonder horse divines.

Mere twitches and quivers, so the lore goes,
gave it all away, betrayed each fresh dupe
until tics spelled out a grainy fate.

Is that why I want to make a half-moon
of that scar? To knead the star
on that huge wise forehead we took turns

patting over the weathered rails
until it's a story fit for a child's bedtime?
A woodchip no larger than an eyelash

leaves a smart blue mark, an inkling,
and it's all I can do to cup my hand
so it will out and our day can end.

# Under Gemini

Starfish the color of peaches,
      apricots. Crabs the size
of our fists. The tide reaches
      and withdraws; our eyes

accustom themselves to the dim
      theater of the pools.
What small worlds. From rim
      to rim, anemones, schools

of tireless minnow, pews
      of mussels. You long
to hold a star but refuse
      temptation. It's wrong

to plunder, wrong to dwell
      on surfaces. But still,
when you spy another shell
      you love—turban, drill,

mother-of-pearl—I fail
      your finger's bidding: the gleam
of your mirrored face arrests. Pale,
      close to ghostly, you seem

for a moment no more real
      than in memory, than you were
last night, westbound, the windshield
      swimming with your sure

features, your easy pleasure
     as the twins emerged.
The heavens cannot be measured.
     Stars and your eyes converged.

# South

It's true what you've heard: the first cattlemen
in these parts ordered brides out of catalogues
the way they might leather saddles or hinges.
Light-boned Dutch girls, their necks ringed
with lace, or the fourth daughter of an Oslo butcher
who never managed to lose her faint odor of roast.
Sharing the dock with the rest of the new arrivals,

the silver and oolong and lashed otter pelts,
they must have peered overhead at the sound
of those insistent winches that turned out
to be hovering gulls after all, and tightened
their fists around the scraps of envelopes
and the smeared ink of impossible instructions.
Next would come the inventing of faces,

cheeks coppered beneath shapeless hats,
faces they would have to learn to trim beards on
and kiss. A prayer in the old language and braids
knotted over again. Then, too soon, the ride south:
the weaving coast route out of the mission town
hewn from wind-drubbed cliffs by platoons of coolies,
the sheer drop you can feel in the pit of your gut

even now, just sightseeing. Such is our history
together, our repeated motions: spars of lore,
vagrant confidences, cautionary tales. It's true
what you've heard. In the dream I plan to have, I'm not
the name on the envelope but the one delivering you;
the one squinting as two horses pick their way upslope
through the ruthless mist this place is famous for.

# Sudden Clarity at the Artichoke Stands

It's the bargain season along the highway
where the valley's steel-wool sky will strip
the milestones off your map. Five for a dollar.
Six for a dollar. Twenty cents a pound.
It's these daylong beading damps,
the locals will tell you, that usher in
the apparitions of ramshackle artichoke huts:
one after another yawing out of the fog,
desperately generous, just before you pass.

The first point to concede to the artichoke
is its fierce erotica. All that opening, armor
that seems to talk you out of it, that covert bud
speaking volumes for everything forbidden.
So much of it prelude. But even here, where they
tumble out of flatbeds, spill over tables,
and lend a wanton air to the roadsides,
it's no different than anywhere else:
the emblems of desire resolve into the particular.
I'm thinking of a checkered tablecloth,
careworn hands, the slow cajoling of blue flame
and a kitchen window hitched six inches
to keep the spices honest. Scarves of steam:
two artichokes perspiring on my mother's china.

I'm thinking of a table at a beachfront café
and the fingers of a woman who sums it all up,
undressing an artichoke with all the deliberacy
of a carefully rehearsed sadness. I still recall
the narrowness of those wrists, teethmarks
on the spent clutter of petals, the last lump

of its heart finding its way into my own mouth:
her quipping gift, her quick parting gesture.

And I'm losing myself, as the scale complains
tunelessly beneath my dozen, over the pluck
it must have taken to first contrive a delicacy
in the prickly conundrum of chain-mail blossoms,
over the artful lengths we go for our three seconds
of shuddering. It is absurd. It is always absurd,
passion, until we abandon ourselves to the
piercing details: Chinese soap, chestnut birthmark
above her left nipple, hole in the armpit
of her favorite dress; Pigeon Point Light, Coltrane,
dusty blackberries in a slumbering culvert;
the alarming lavender sky in the Monet postcard
pinned at perfect eye-level to one who is
leaning close, looking up, taking her.

# Small Hours

When the dark is wise to us, what is memory
But what the body agrees to abide by?
What comes upon us in a rush? Afterwards,
She talked and he listened. It was the year
Of her birth. The melons were prodigious
That summer, and the heat off the charts.
She likes the story best about her father
Fishtailing into a farmstand lot to purchase
A historic watermelon, thumping it gravely
With a knuckle before hugging it to his chest,
Though the contractions by that time
Were fierce. She likes the thought
Of newspapers spread on the tailgate
All delivery long. The Rambler parked
In the shade by the hospital. Her father
Slicing away. An overpowering sweetness.
She got out of bed to open the window.
Her body was darker than the rest of the room.
Then he talked and she listened. He likes
How inside the lumpishness of melons
Brightness waits like a seemly thought
Right before the tongue fleshes it out.
The way it lurks. The way it takes us back.
If loving is always groping in the dark,
If the heart keeps us on tenterhooks,
Then at times the body we find beside us
Will be the only steady source of light
At the back of the cave. He doesn't like
To call it a shining or a glowing.

It's more tacit than that. More ulterior.
Root and vine, bed and spade, curve and heft.
Something opens and we see.

# The Earth Is Round

In your absence, I lean
Into the wind, linger beside
The fields and ditches across the tracks,
Tear up shaggy handfuls of sweet grass
To please the broodmares. Burrs alight
On my coat. Cabbage butterflies
Blunder against my face, seek out
My ears. Coming home, I disappear
Up to my waist in bone-dry annuals.
Who is so companionable, so sure of love,
As to resist the blandishments
Of waning summer? I shake my head
In front of the hall mirror—half in jest,
Half in wonder—and watch
Dandelion-haze and thistle-fuzz fly.
I pluck foxtails out of my socks.
It wins me over, all this impetuosity,
The skill and conviction with which
The passing season pins its hopes on me.
There must be spores and spendthrift kernels
In my cuffs, winged pods in my pockets,
Pollen-dust spirited into the air
When my lashes flutter. Yes, it must
Be so, now that the last of the wildflowers
Have perished. *Gone to seed,*
We say, in tacit deprecation, but who
Among us gives up the ghost
In measures any more exacting?
Milkweed turns loose its plumed spurs
In the faintest breeze, and newly hatched
Spiders, in May, sail across lawns

And public gardens on audacious
Silver threads. And a man and woman
Who drifted off beneath the honeylocusts
Wake in a snarl of glistening silk
And share a moment's laughter about
What binds them, what keeps them close.

# Autumnal Primer

In the oak glades high above the classrooms
an impromptu exercise in enchantment:
*chanterelle*, she declaimed, prince among fungi.
And there they were, hanging fire in the loam

like the spotlit coins a conjuror can pluck
from our very ears. Repeat after me,
*chanterelle*: so prized among French country folk
hunting parties comb the woods with harnessed swine.

Congeries of lumpish caps, clustered thrusts
of lucid delicacies conjugated out of rot.
Fairy rings, she explained: quorums mustered
after soakings, each crop rekindling its legend.

And on she pressed, blazing the route,
singing out upon each fresh discovery.
*Chanterelle*, she called. *Chandelier*, I shouted back.
I cupped my earth-caked hands: *chanteuse*.

Who could say where incantation ended
and incandescence began? So reigned
the wantonness of nomenclature; so went
the gleaning of those neon-honey mushrooms.

Truants, repeat after me: slice the flesh crosswise
into aureoles and doubloons. Sauté briskly
and season to taste before any of you remember
to keep a civil tongue in your head.

# Studebaker Luck

Later, when it all went wrong, we called it
Studebaker luck, after the carapace
Of the touring car stuck fast in the marsh
Like a locust immured in primeval amber.
The candy-apple body gone to rust
Was our home-made paradigm of misfortune,
The backseat nodding with cattails,
Each cavernous headlight a nest of coot.

If the light was right and the water low,
We could spot it from the bedroom window.
A touchstone of stigma. An enduring shambles.
We imagined a family late for a picnic,
A father's hands like hams on the wheel,
Or a young couple courting disaster,
Defying the antique curfew of their day.
We imagined it spring, the frogs in tune.

By midsummer, your version favored
Everything unexceptional. The country doctor
On a call for mumps. Someone's botched notion
Of the scenic route. A day unmarred by
Rain or intrigue, a basking afternoon
When reflexes relaxed. Who knew otherwise?
For every tragic joyride, there's scores of wrecks
Where everyone walks away without a scratch.

Here we had it. A landmark that spoke for
All that's unsalvageable. That steering wheel

Ravished with ages of moss was evidence
That there's nothing arresting or uncommon
About eyes straying, detours so obscure
They're irresistable, remorseless swerves.
That ravaged facade of showroom chrome
Was proof that nature abhors a boomtime.

Later, when an umber tedium left you ripe
For undisguised infidelities, we called it
Studebaker luck. A proverbial fluke.
Later still, as the scales tipped, we saw
Studebaker luck at work. The brutal winter.
The rise in roadkill deer. The icy morning
When the marshlight surprised the shards
Of every mirror and piece of china in the place.

# Talking Cure

Troubled souls, if you will, must sleep by craft.
One I shared a bed with for a spell would find a seat
On the Northern Crescent Line night in,
Night out, as soon as she closed her eyes.

She began with what she knew: upcountry hometown,
Belle époque station, the one-armed custodian
Killing time with an indolent broom. In her mind
The platform milled with the hubbub of departure

And bodies unlocking after last farewells.
Then that lurch, that shriek. That telling rhythm.
First to slip by were the rowhouses, then cramped backyards,
And she always waited for a certain picket fence

On which two girls in pinafores always perched
And faithfully waved. The train would snake alongside
The river's oxbows; the river was named for a minor saint;
The name of the saint was flaking off the water tower.

My presence, she told me, prolonged the journey.
She knew it would be one of those nights she ran out
Of riverfront and lowland, the smokestacks and warehouses
She had by heart, one of those nights she had to shift

All her attention to the interior of the compartment.
That meant more intricacy, more finegrained devisings:
The muffled slap of an endless gin game, the cherry tang
Of pipesmoke in defiance of code, the peacock feather

Flaring from a matron's hat in a risible arabesque.
And then the subtext of her choice: perhaps a rhubarb
Over misplaced luggage and lamentable manners,
Perhaps a father reading aloud to his son, the son

Breaking in with imperious questions, the father exacting
And evasive by turns, the story resuming once again.
Sometimes she'd banter with the passenger beside her.
Sometimes she'd begin a wobbly letter to her sister.

That sister, it turned out, was one of the waving girls.
She was the other one. I was another in a series of men
Hitched end to end, if you will, as the nights ground on
And the platform thronged and her breath honed its edge.

If I ever inferred the nature of what plagued her,
It's forgotten. If I clutched her in a clumsy gesture
More than once, it's been erased. But if I bear her in mind,
I know it will come to me—the name of the river

And the town, that third-string pinewoods saint,
The lettering still peeling after all this time
On the water tower you can spot from the train.
I will begin the retouching with my customary firmness:

An admirable shade of imperial blue, let's say,
Crisply trimmed with white; a dip and a downstroke,
A downstroke and a dip, the same circumspect
And implicit mechanics I've employed so often

For the stenciled capitals of phantom storefront glass.
I will lay down as many coats as it takes.
It's a trick I have, a technique I can depend on
When the minute hand churns and it gets so awfully late.

# The Threshers

Observed too briskly, this could well be combat:
twin figures squared off with arms outstretched,
each shifting into the downstroke of a vehement blow

that means to relieve the rival of his head.
A pardonable error, for who of us knows a flail
when we see one, that odd implement come down to us

in the garb of a verb? It looks like a cross
between a hockey stick and a carpenter's square,
but swung just so, it served famously for those who beat

wheat from chaff, as the saying goes—though if accuracy
is what we crave, it's best to speak of flogging out
kernel and seed from husks and stems. That's what's meant

at the root by *threshing*, and that's what the woodcut
is illustrating, shrunk to the size of a postage stamp
beside the citation in my antiquated unabridged.

So they do not intend to brain each other, after all,
these foursquare characters, the threshers. They are toiling
in unison, flailing a sketchy mound of grain

strewn across the entrance of a rustic structure
(the threshold!), ushering in a representative autumn
in the early 19th century. No doubt they timed their strokes

with seasoned aplomb, wise to the other's arc and swath.
A crackerjack duo must have struck a clockwork groove.
Securely bucolic, their industry cannot entirely escape

an undercurrent of ruthlessness: the grip on the shaft
says the lash is the gist. The tendentious English tongue
saw to it this strain assumed the upper hand

when the vowel began to shift—thus, whosoever will *thrash*
calls up the ghost of the brute force such men mustered
to whip ripe wheat, to drub the summer crop.

Noah Webster's myrmidons counsel us that it's proper
either way, but surely they're behind the curve.
Anyone beset with garden-variety night sweats can thrash,

but threshers are an utterly uprooted breed, dumbstruck,
their exertions embalmed in figures of speech.
It's like getting a postcard from a suburb of Babel,

having them materialize like this, throwbacks
to the grit-caked literal instance underwriting the idiom,
the palpable heft and sinew beneath what learned heads

of the day were wont to call "the dress of thought."
So much for sweeping language, then: let me stress
their innate stick-to-itiveness, the sweat of their brow,

their exacting stamina that might still be aptly emulated
by all who hope to lay to rest appearances of conflict
by mulling it over, working it through, thrashing it out.

# The Anatomy of Complicity

Another Sunday, loom of shadow on the pillow,
        he watches a spider for a good full hour
laboring above them in the open window.

The night had proven too warm, and waking
        in a mild sweat, he'd eased the pane
as high as it would go. The sky was breaking

into curious bands of silver, ashen pinks,
        and the distant pulse of the radio tower
assumed a disconsolate air. And to think

that before the morning was nearly spent,
        sill and window would be sutured skein
by skein with coolly murderous intent!

He finds it strangely agreeable, strangely pleasing.
        His mind plays over the themes of design
and chance, considers how the seizing

of opportunity naturally had to precede
        the fastidious spinning. And it occurs
to him that his plans to mow and weed

and rake the yard might wait another week.
        Let the leaves lie where they fall, let the vine
snake up the drainpipe! He brushes the flushed cheek

of his sleeping wife, runs lingering fingertips
        over the traceries of leaves and branches astir
on the rumpled sheet. He reaches up and snaps

the radio on—a lambent counterpoint for strings
        and continuo brims the narrow room.
Is this tranquility or indolence? How many things

must be denied their flourishing, quashed in a flash,
        if one is ever to call a life one's own?
Sweat of one's brow, yes, thorns in the flesh—

yet what a frail reed is the scruple that gives
        no quarter to pockets of unaccountable calm
in the ambit of the mundane, those little reprieves

from brute ambition when the self seems to twirl
        by a thread. The web is radiant: can one remain
steadfast while embracing the snares of the world?

# The Tapestry Gallery

The handbook's glosses are lucid, yet the prized tableaux
bristling with heraldry and iconography, signs and wonders,
always appear imperiled, very nearly overcome

by the fields and gardens and lavish woodland prospects
that teem with the Old World's natural history:
herbs and flowers so closely observed, so sharply rendered,

we can still name them, lean hounds with flaming tongues
and a glimmering concordance of native songbirds
splicing every copse and thicket, globed pears and quinces

clustered just out of reach. How easily the storyline is lost
amid the delirious filigree and flourishing profusion!
Unless, as he'd like to tell her this time, one allows

the weave itself to be the rightful narrative:
the needlework that's every bit as patient and alert
in the tufted down of a spring hare's ear

and the sprigs of wild rosemary pricking up underfoot
and the spurt of pearl on a quail's plush breast
as in the freighted gaze of the ivory unicorn, jackknifing

to watch the lance sink in. Unless, descending
the stairs with her at closing time, detecting a new strand
of silver in her hair, he at last resolves

that the allegory cannot be perennially revived,
the loom's riddles unraveled, the emblematic counterpoint
of legend and doctrine brought to life—

only the quality of light, the intensity of particulars,
the strain of scrupulous embellishment that promises,
from every angle, to engulf the field of vision.

# The Favor

Wear that pearl necklace of your mother's
        for me tonight. Seeing our flaws
                in others often embitters us,

I know, but I'm sure I would have loved
        your father precisely for his famous
                ingenuousness, and his willingness,

always, to be deceived. Yes,
        he paid hundreds for a rosary
                of fetching imitations, but it was

years and years before anyone
        was the wiser—and all the while,
                I imagine, it must have been

an endless source of pleasure
        for him to picture those avid divers
                sporting like dolphins in the wave

of the proprietor's hand, plunging smartly,
        time and again, from spidery piers,
                and looting the bottoms

of turquoise coves, just so the woman
        he never stopped courting
                might look a little lovelier,

Saturday evenings, on his arm.
        And you cannot tell me
                he was cheated, his devotion

cheapened by this string of lies.
        For in his eyes, I'm sure,
                by candlelight, by streetlamp,

by the dim aquarium glow
        of the shuddering streetcar
                bearing them home, this luster

spoke for everything left unsaid
        between them, for words that would
                have rung false. Gather the hair now

up off of your neck, so I can
        hook the clasp, not to ask
                that history repeat itself,

exactly, but so as to see ourselves
        in light of generous notions
                of consequence and consent,

shared error and forbearance,
        which so often, I'm persuaded,
                adorn favorably entwined lives.